Walking Between the Raindrops

Walking Between the Raindrops

Poems by

Thomas DeFreitas

© 2025 Thomas DeFreitas. All rights reserved.
This material may not be reproduced in any form, published,
reprinted, recorded, performed, broadcast,
rewritten, or redistributed without
the explicit permission of Thomas DeFreitas.
All such actions are strictly prohibited by law.

Cover design by Shay Culligan
Cover photo by Jack Finnigan via Unsplash
Author photo by Leaman Corkum

ISBN: 978-1-63980-704-8
Library of Congress Control Number: 2025932423

Kelsay Books
502 South 1040 East, A-119
American Fork, Utah 84003
Kelsaybooks.com

for Julia Fehrenbacher
with splashy superabundant gratitude

I hear you. I see you. Me too.

Acknowledgments

Autumn Sky Poetry Daily: "Rhyme Past My Prime," "Grief," "Reconciliation"
The Beehive Anthology of Arlington Poets: "Blessed Space," "Poem at Dawn"
Boston Area Small Press and Poetry Scene: "One Day at a Time" (as "Day at a Time")
Changes & Chances: "Left Field," "Starlight," "Rochambo," [as "Sunlight in Milwaukee"], "Dean Amy," "Confession with Jennifer"
Ovunque Siamo: "111th Letter to Elena," "God"
Pensive: "A Look Askance at Spring"
The Pilgrim: "Left Field"
Poetry Porch: "At Half Past Five" (as "Quarter Past Five"), "Paulist Center," "Vespers," "This Day Just Past"
Red Letter Poems: "Where the Words Come From" (the series, available by email subscription, is curated and circulated by Steven Ratiner, former poet laureate of Arlington, MA)

*

"Grief" received a nomination for a 2024 Pushcart Prize by the editor of *Autumn Sky Poetry Daily.*

*

Sincerest thanks to Kelsay Books for publishing this, my fourth collection with the publisher! Special acknowledgments are due to Karen Kelsay, Olivia Loftis, and Jenna Wray. Big thanks to Shay Culligan for his solicitous attention to cover design.

Warmest acknowledgments to Linda Haviland Conte, to Julia Fehrenbacher, and to jojo Lazar for their kind words on the back cover, by which I am graced and gladdened.

I'm grateful to Christine Klocek-Lim for her input on an early draft of "After My First Visit." Thanks to Faith Blake for a suggestion about "This Unbidden Love," a suggestion which I have cheerfully adopted!

Sincerest esteem and deep affection to Hilary Sallick and Mary Buchinger, my big sisters in poetry. With profoundest respect, I acknowledge the four poets laureate of Arlington, Massachusetts: Miriam Levine (2015–17), Cathie Desjardins (2017–19), Steven Ratiner (2019–22), and Jean Flanagan (2023–present).

Shout-out to everyone at St James's Episcopal Church, in Cambridge, Massachusetts: that sacred space is very much my home. Blessings upon the luminous humans of The Crossing, who convene at the Cathedral Church of St. Paul in Boston; new to your circle, I am fortified by you unfailingly.

Alisha, Ashley, BBB, Debba, Donna, Elena, Elizabeth, Emily, Heather, Ingrid, Jet, John, LauraLai, Lisa, Steven: sending you the big gratitudes and all the wacky graces.

To Mom, my steadiest supporter: much love, many hugs, all the blessings. To all family members who have celebrated my publications: I am immeasurably grateful. Memory eternal to Dad, to Elaine ("Bangum"), to Cousin Sue ("The Bishop"), and to dear friend Jen, whose loss I still feel keenly. You shine as inextinguishable stars in my spiritual firmament.

To all who are reading this book: peace and light.

Contents

1 Where the Words Come From

This Unbidden Love	17
Contributor's Note	18
For John Clare	19
Speak Again, Bright Angel	20
New Directions Paperbook 316	21
Eighties Soundtrack	23
Poem at Dawn	24
Left Field	25
One Day at a Time	26
Starlight	28
Where the Words Come From	29

2 Milwaukee & So Forth

Wisconsin Winter	33
Your Milwaukee	34
Abide	35
After My First Visit	37
How I Wish	40
111th Letter to Elena	41
Rochambo	42

3 Sonnets & Songs

Buffalo Nickels & Clear Skies Above	45
Rhyme Past My Prime	46
Maybe, Just Maybe	48
Grief	49
At Half Past Five	50
Paulist Center	51
Vespers	52

This Day Just Past	53
Dean Amy	54
Hymn: Wisdom	55
Hymn: Her Name Is Grace	56

4 A Candle in the Gathering Gloom

A Look Askance at Spring	59
Daughters	60
Amid Cold Churches	61
Confession with Jennifer	62
Reconciliation	63
God	64
Portrait of the Oddest	65
Chestnut Street Episode	66
Blessed Space	67
Nightpiece	68
What Is Love?	69

1

Where the Words Come From

This Unbidden Love

    The least conceivable
      flower that ever will have grown:
late April's lilac of pervasive scent,
its clustered petals shaken by the wind,
    a breath alive, a flesh unknown,
        a world springlike and full.

    The ripest sweetest fruit
      turned liquid on the swirling tongue
becomes a wine-drunk whisper tasting loud,
revives forgotten midnights in the gut,
    and bitter sinful saccharines
        stimulate the tooth.

    Two souls, four lungs: each nerve
      breathes fulfillment of its dream
while this unbidden love, the tide's great surge,
turbulent ecstasy of rapturous urge,
    makes thrive, in one climactic rhyme,
        the pinnacle of sense.

Contributor's Note

Thomas DeFreitas
is a professional sluggard
and spelling-bee champion emeritus.

Gifted with a freakishly
accurate memory for birthdays,
he enjoys ravioli,
dead squid,
and the sonnets of Trumbull Stickney.

He is not the lead singer
of the alternative band
Single Use Plastics.
For over thirty years,
Los Angeles, California
has not been his home.

His poems have not appeared
in the following small magazines:
*Kinesis, Kenosis, Necrosis,
Tear Down This Mall.*

DeFreitas writes:
"I am interested in the spirituality
of the early Cistercian
Guerric of Igny.
I also like Save Ferris's cover
of 'Come On, Eileen.'"

For John Clare

I love to see leaves blaze red,
their yellow veins making pale streaks;
see squirrels scamper up broad-shouldered oaks,
or the dun-gray rabbit with its milk-white tail
(long-eared big-bellied bag of bounce and frisk)
happily loping from picket fence to path.

I love the moon distinct in the sky's deep blue
making the blueness all around it glow.

I love to see frost crisp and whiten grass,
to hear the clamorous grammar of sparrows
half-bicker and half-praise in the newborn light.

I love to drink fresh water, achingly cold,
in cupped and lifted hands (the lively water
that rushes over slick stones of the Gale)—
and most of all, on cold November nights,
I love the smell of unseen threads of woodsmoke
from a neighbour's fire in the year's huddled dusk.

Speak Again, Bright Angel

about the language of love

Whenever she curses the *verkakte* computer,
or calls someone a pain in the *tuchas,*
or tells me, "you look *oysgeshpilt,* Tommo:
geh schlafen, geh schlafen"—

then oak-trees start to belly-dance;
then withered roses blush and bloom;
then Spy Pond's water turns to champagne!

Then birds of the air, then fish of the sea,
whatsoever walketh or swimmeth or flieth,
fin and feather and flesh, all exult and sing
hosanna, hosanna in the highest—

and the voice of the turtle awakes once more
in a land famished for grace.

My breviary,
my Book of Common Prayer
when I was young and easy,
the best instruction manual I ever had
for learning my craft and sullen art,
I carried you everywhere
in all kinds of weather.

The sharp edges of your pages
softened with the wear of the elements
and my incessant thumbing.

As you began to fall apart,
I kept you together
with innumerable little ribbons
of Scotch tape.

I drank from you
deep draughts of lyric moonshine.
I loved you like the frosty fingers
of dark October wind.

East Boston kids would ask me,
"Who's *Dye*-lin Thomas?"
My corrections, if you'll forgive me,
did not go gentle!

I still quote from you,
chapter and verse,
at the drop of a spondee.

I still hear the raven
cough in winter sticks.

I still feel the force
that through the green fuse
drives flowers of fire—
the bard of Laugharne
brandy and ripe
in his bright eternal prime.

Eighties Soundtrack

We snuggled ugly, you and I,
under the lampposts of Noddle Island in August.
We gobbled *Hitchhiker's Guide,* played Depeche Mode,
until September deep-sixed our adventures.

We *lived,* we did. Wrestled, wrote poems, dozed,
feckless and dopey amid stiff triple-deckers,
subversive sophomores in a sensual summer,
daffodils in the boxing ring, monks at the circus.

Mope-rock symphonies, falsetto sobs:
Sparkle in the Rain. Low-life. Hatful of Hollow.
You've run off with my reason, split with my wits,
jaybird of the fire-plugs, buxom bundle of whim!

Poem at Dawn

Be still, and let
morning happen.

Let dark blue foredawn
brighten into day.
Let traffic occur,
let coffee brew.

Let mind be lively,
eyes awake
to many newnesses.

Let commerce begin,
and contemplation.

Let the gravestones
of Mount Pleasant Cemetery
whiten in the rising light.

And though it is still
technically winter,
let the tender flower
of this young moment
unfold and open
to the fullness of spring.

Let the shrinking patches
of tired old snow
trickle away into *yester*—
into *ago*.

Left Field

In left field
of the schoolkids' ballpark
two old men sit
on collapsible chairs
in mellow October sun
and have a tête-à-tête
about heaven knows what

they are not rushed
they are not bitter
they seem aloof
from opinions
and other urgencies

as I walk past them
my own heart gladdened
by their evident gladness

I think
there's a poem here

maybe even a prayer

One Day at a Time

April 2020

Pent-up by fear of what prowls
microscopically through open air,
felling the feeble, rattling the robust,
I pace from corner to corner
of my cluttered two-room flat,
where poems multiply like dust-bunnies,
where worries go viral,
where rumors of wakening leaflife
seep in through drafts around the bedroom window.

I'm eager for that happy evening
weeks or months from now
when once more I can hug
the weary fellow members
of my folding-chair fraternity,
serene, courageous, wise, or trying to be.

Battle-scarred veterans
of long wars against themselves
who brush away self-pity in a newbie
with "Tough shit, kiddo, just don't pick up."

I miss the quarts of coffee
brewed with inept enthusiasm,
strong enough to peel paint.

I miss the Oreos and Chips Ahoy.

I miss the truck-drivers who drop F-bombs
and dangerous women in knee-high boots
who drop refreshing honesty
and make the truckers blush.

Sure, there's the laptop screen
bradybunching e-meetings
into our cozy homes.

But I look forward to the day
when I can ride the bus
as it crawls down car-clotted avenues
to get me to the basement of St Peter's Church
just in time for the moment of silence.

Starlight

When I could no longer
stomach the preachiness
of the old-timers' shares,
I slipped out of the basement
of Our Lady of Lourdes Church
and walked into the parking lot
under immaculate starlight.
A February night just cold enough
to bring me back to life.
I said my Joyful Mysteries
on a set of small black beads.

I stood facing the church
and a stained-glass rendering
of Bernadette and Our Lady
faintly illumined from within.

Where the Words Come From

my prayer
is cold sunlight
on forsythia

as the cooke's hollow brook
burbles and gushes
in the background

as a lone sparrow
bounces along
hard new england soil

like the consonants
in the verb *pipiabat*
(pipe and chirrup

of his lover's pet
in that poem
by catullus)

my prayer
is the slouch and slack
of sleepless nights

at the laptop
as i write to a friend
and wonder

where the words come from

2
Milwaukee & So Forth

Wisconsin Winter

Milwaukee bus-stop,
subzero chill,
steamy air
from a sidewalk grate.

Two commuters
happily met
share the square
as they wait.

And wait.

Your Milwaukee

In cyber-mail or hand-penned letter,
describe the baristas
of Stone Creek and of Rochambo,
the Wifi'd customers in suit, in sweater,
casual as friends, or stiff as barristers.

Give me Wisconsin
with birds of finest feather!
Sketch your spot
in the square where sparrows gather
for crumbs and contention.

Send me petals as they emerge:
daffodil, crocus, hydrangea,
forsythia and leaves on the verge
of their greenest growing.
Tell me how your family's doing.

Let me see the mirror and rail
of your dance class, the swivelly chair
of your office in the twelve-story tower.
Sandwiches at your lunch hour.
Raspberry Spindrift. Ginger ale.

Write to me as the sly stars wink
or when the sun yawns, half awake:
invite me, please! into your Milwaukee;
let me join you for a cup of coffee
at Rochambo or at Stone Creek.

Abide

I've raised my thermostat to 76:
outside in the dark before dawn, it's twelve above.

Naomi has counselled me to pry myself
from the clutches of caffeine.

I'm looking at the washed and drying dishes in my kitchen
to see if there's a poem
among the spoons and cereal bowls.

Banks and bluffs of snow harden in the freeze.
I might venture outside today
for the first time since Wednesday.

A lettered and laurelled professor
once urged a friend of mine
never to put a question in a poem.
How silly! Where would Oliver and Roethke be
without their life-giving questions?

*

One in the afternoon:
I hear the sore-throated scrape of snowplows,
the litany of beeps when they back up.

I finished the bag of tortilla chips I started last night.

Temperature's risen to 26.
I've lowered the thermostat. But not by much.

Sun-glare, ice-glare. As I look outside,
my eyes cringe from this whiteness,
this graceless insistence, this stridency of light.

My sight would shelter in the candle-dotted dark
of an ancient monastery's chapel.

I would seek refuge in the cathedral's sanctuary
where Jennifer laid hands upon my head
as I knelt before her to hear her pronounce
words of absolution: *Thomas, abide in peace.*

After My First Visit

I praise JetBlue, five, six miles high,
zipping me across the glacial æther!
De-planing, I smile at the pilot and announce,
"My first flight in 45 years!"
He deadpans, "Mine too."

I celebrate scrambled eggs, bacon, and multigrain toast
at Rocket Baby on North in Wauwatosa.
I applaud the sprawl and shade of a low-branched tree
(you'll know which kind) at Atwater Beach.

We'd still be enjoying sandwiches on the sandy blanket
were it not for those hornets—
not many of them, and thank God they didn't jab us.

And oh, those little swindlers near the University—
lemonade-stand con-men, four-flushing grade-schoolers!
They took three dollars of mine
for a plastic bracelet worth at most twenty cents.
Well and good. Capitalism must continue!

*

A guest in your home, I am both stiff and silly.
I am ushering in a new "error" of presidential impressions.
I plan to fling confetti at Ted's Ice Cream
and shout "Wowzers!" at the stained glass of Trinity.

Thank you, Elena, for blessing my nervous eagerness:
I would be butler and busboy
to your every breakfast and dinner.

I will bow to calendar years
etched into the concrete of Milwaukee sidewalks.
Describing I-94, I will say "rowt" instead of "root."
I will cheer for Team Catbird.

I'll solace the tired Black ladies on the 21,
the cumbrous bus harrumphing along
past liquor stores, Baptist churches, the Matt Talbot Lodge.

Next time I come to the 414,
I'll bring students with clipboards and favourite causes—
we have a crop of them near Harvard Book Store.
I'll plant a few near Boswell's and Stone Creek.

*

My whimsy sits
on the sand-white shores of Lake Michigan:
cormorant in a milk-crate, seagull on a Zoom-grid.

My exuberance blooms, my joy is Queen Anne's lace
as I walk, acrophobic,
across the boardwalk of Marsupial Bridge.

Elena, let me spend four days and three nights
in the dominion of women who persist;
let me abide in Freya's hospitable haven,
let me linger in the realm of sausage and tortellini.

You have given me neon signs for Blatz Beer,
you have graced me with leafleted coffee-shops,
you have brought me Rochambo
on the last Thursday of August.

*

You give me the meandering tendril
of a hanging plant with a single pink aster.

You are the *raison d'être* of all things smiling and sage,
you who delve and dive into dense yellow lexicons:
yours is the counsel I heed: your decrees, bright and benign.

You place fresh flowers on the night-table,
golden petals, petals of rusty red.

And yes, the five-panelled painting you have made!—
moonlight, dark sky, winter-stripped tree-branch,
hush of settling snow on December's secret sabbath.

How I Wish

I could have holed up
in a Wisconsin monastery
& never come back to Boston

how I wish I could have spent centuries
in your congenial precincts
with coffee & soup & Wauwatosa
& walks across Marsupial Bridge

how I wish I could have stayed
where the tenor of life was gentle
where the voices inside me were kind

*

explain me this   dear poetfriend

why can I not abide in a heaven
where all the angels have sonnets for wings
& flimsy dimestore plastic ankle-bracelets
on which are written proverbs of compassion

lead me to rivers of crystal-throated music
take me to pastures bright with morning-glories

111th Letter to Elena

A few notches after four
in the miscalled morning.
A dark wind howls.

Have you lately considered the stars?
The word "consider" contains stars,
as you likely know. *Sidera,*
plural, neuter, third declension.

The doughnut shop across the street
opens in less than an hour. I might go
say hello to Sophia, to Kenya,
to the Brazilian woman whose shrieking voice
is the Ides of March to my nerves and spine.
I'll grab a cup of mud and sit awhile.

And then, afterwards, I might linger
under the sky, which wears black longer
so close to the colder solstice,
and I'll stand, I'll tarry under the stars
that give me courage, "strange courage"
as they shine, so steady and resolute,
so swerveless and imperturbable,
upon our fractious and fractured world.

Rochambo

a coffeehouse in East Milwaukee

Sunlight in Milwaukee sparkles rivers.
And on East Brady, past the old Blatz sign,
stands coffeed Rochambo with stiff-backed chairs.

I totter as I climb the narrow stairs
up to the second floor. We sit and plan—
grab the 21 back over the river?

I talk too much, but your attentive ears
don't seem to mind my gab. I'm on Cloud Ten
as we sip cold soft drinks in facing chairs!

Last day of August. Summer hasn't wavered
in its brash strut, its blare of blinding sun.
Light floods Milwaukee, dazzles its three rivers.

What stroke of luck, what grace or fate togethers
two long-time cyber-pals? At last, I've seen
the Kwan Yin statuette, the painted chairs.

Dear poetfriend, let's vow not to be strangers:
next April or next May, let's meet again;
you'll lead me over the Milwaukee River
to Rochambo, its tables and its chairs.

3

Sonnets & Songs

Buffalo Nickels & Clear Skies Above

Daisies and doorknobs, cathedrals and parasols:
All these and more I deliver with love!
Icicles, bicycles, Thanksgiving dinner-plates,
Buffalo nickels and clear skies above.

Rain-polished cobblestones. Lush grass to walk upon.
Bright petals tossed at your glorious tread.
Hyacinths. Asteroids. Comets and daffodils.
Garlands of gladness to circle your head.

Off-color anecdotes. Whimsical whisperings.
Lilac-perfume on a late April breeze.
All of my cheerfully abject obedience
Offered to you as I bend both my knees.

Bottle-caps, mandolins, ice-cream and ticket-stubs,
Swan-boats and harps in a vale of delight.
Countesses, courtiers. Book-ends and bobolinks.
Dollar-store flip-flops. A cool autumn night.

Denim-clad majesty, fizz in my seltzer, my
Diva of threescore, my cool turtle-dove!
Bergman and Bogart in my *Casablanca,* you're
Buffalo nickels, you're clear skies above.

Rhyme Past My Prime

after W. H. Auden's "Doggerel by a Senior Citizen"

Our earth in 2023
is quite the atmosphere for me,
a dancer at the roped-off door
of Studio (Birthday) 54.

Some politicians—O my Lord!—
cause me to pine for Gerald Ford;
and radio's loud cacophonies
make me miss Prince, the Cars, and Squeeze.

My friend Deb watches films and such:
I'm desperately out of touch.
She'll say the name of some bright pup
with a Golden Globe. I can't keep up.

I'm not a man inclined to grovel
before the NYT's top novel.
Though it may speak of faded promise,
I'm still fanboy for Dylan Thomas.

Gen Z, in all their pride and finery,
shake off confinement to the binary:
I listen, with embracing ear,
to grow in love that casts out fear.

Religion's rife with traps and snares,
but still, each night, I say my prayers
to Blessed Grace in heaven's palace.
I hope She'll keep me free from malice.

Recurrently, among the tedia,
I find myself on Social Media,
commenting, liking, cracking jokes
with Swedish, French, Australian folks.

Pandora, Bandcamp, Spotify
bewilder me. I don't know why!
It's YouTube Premium for me,
the closest thing to MTV.

I make allowances for Kindle,
but when my battery starts to dwindle,
I'll search for a convenient socket—
then pull a book from shelf or pocket.

My hair these days has gone as grey
as Wystan Auden's clogged ashtray,
but every twenty-four, I start
with supple soul, accepting heart.

So, from my outpost north of Boston,
I bless this world I'm often lost in.
I'll fumble till I get things right
and strive to live by peace and light.

Maybe, Just Maybe

Woman of kind heart and of tear-tired eyes,
of dark hair dashed with gray, of forthright speech,
compassionate soul by many trials grown wise,
I want to learn all that you have to teach.

I'd like to help you, deep in your distress:
I'd soothe your nettled brow, I'd kneel beside
those weary and well-travelled feet to bless
the ground made holy by your tender tread.

I long to be the one who binds your wounds,
who mitigates your pain, eases your hurt,
who listens to you as day-labour ends,
and evening comes at last to heal the heart.

And maybe, just maybe, once in a while,
I'd be that face at whom you choose to smile.

Grief

Grief is the heart feeling a phantom limb:
estrangement's bitter wine, wept memory,
the loss that never will unlose itself,
departure from which there is no return.

It is the strain of music cut off just
as the crescendo starts to swell and gather.
It is the thousand texts and conversations
that never will take place except in dreams.

Grief is five white knuckles shaken at God,
the prayer refusing in its rage to pray,
the rosary of memories rehearsed

as if remembering could raise the dead,
as if the loved and lost could breathe again
through the defiant will of the bereaved.

At Half Past Five

At half past five (a.m.), I greeted Lisa
my neighbour smoking in the parking lot
just outside our building. I crossed the street
to get a sausage sandwich at the Dunkin'.

The donutista knows me now by sight,
remembers what I order. She asked first,
in case I had a surprise in store for her.
Horribly predictable. If it ain't broke!

Then Brenda who works at the Book Rack
dropped into Dunks for her morning joe
and maybe a honey-dipped, I couldn't see.

Skies were dark, but the town was waking up.
Trucks rumbled down the Parkway, shook the stars.
I sat and looked out. Foredawn gratitude.

Paulist Center

I went into the Paulist Center chapel
a half-hour-plus before their midday Mass.
I found a woman, fiftyish and barefoot,
pacing calmly, absorbed in unseen light.

Her knee-high boots, her bags, and other things
were clustered by a sideways-facing pew.
Without self-consciousness, she crossed the space
with steady, slow, deliberating tread.

Opposite where she prayed, I found a place
to sit and contemplate Sustaining Grace
made visible in her, my even-Christian.

After several minutes, I got up and walked
across the chapel to Our Lady's corner.
The woman smiled at me. And I smiled back.

Vespers

Cooke's Hollow is my Book of Common Prayer:
its gnarled and skimp-leaved trees, my psalmody;
the mirthy burble of the old mill brook
a litany of grace and gratitude.

Forsythia sings its yellow alleluia
to robin, bluejay, oriole, and sparrow.
And *let us pray* urges the splashless glide
of green-necked mallards as they paddle past.

This meagre strip of nature, snagged between
police headquarters and the Eversource plant:
my chapel *en plein air,* where I can sweep

brain-haze and cobwebs, nettles from my head,
rest for a spell, and watch the ribbon of water
whiten as it twists and rushes by.

This Day Just Past

This day just past: revivifying breezes,
and sunlight's uninjurious clemency!
No, not a day of snow-blast, no deep freezes:
instead, blue sky as far as sight could see.

And now, my starlight-habits! Thought and toil:
poetry, caffeine, rosary, YouTube.
Word-craft. Word-art. My shelter in turmoil.
George Herbert's verse. A glimmer in the gloom.

This morning I might go to Black Seed, chill—
see James Parker, John Lane, & Christie Towers.
Connection. Grace and gift. In a few hours,
I'll have to go to Walgreens, pick up pills:

need milk and bread, and paper napkins, too.
Elena! I should mail her books, and soon.

Dean Amy

In summer showers, winter squalls,
    Be Boston warm or brisk,
I'll go and pray at Old Saint Paul's:
    It's Anglican/Episc.

The Dean of this Cathedral Church
    Is one Amy McCreath:
You'll hardly find, although you search,
    A more outstanding priest.

She's quick to help the down-and-out,
    To lift the poor in spirit;
She'll speak a word dispelling doubt,
    And blest are those who hear it!

The good in everyone she sees
    (Some partisans annoy her):
The Massachusetts Diocese
    Rejoices to employ her!

Though demagogues be coarse and vile,
    Though viruses would slay me,
My heart exults to glimpse the smile
    Of Tremont Street's Dean Amy.

Hymn: Wisdom

Praise, my soul, how Wisdom teaches,
    Gently leading us to grace,
Probing heaven's farthest reaches,
    Delving into inner space:
Let all smooth and stumbling speeches
    Praise the kindness of her face.

Praise, my heart, the wit and reason
    Of her bright discerning eyes;
She creates in every season,
    Blesses us with fresh surprise.
Magnify her lasting brilliance—
    Gracious light that never dies.

Praise the mellow meditations
    She produces in our thought;
Praise her wholesome inspirations
    Granted even when unsought.
Praise her sacred estimations,
    Setting pride and pomp at naught.

Sing out loud with joyful measure
    What Sophia sees and knows:
Let us thank her for the treasure
    Which unstinting she bestows:
Sing to her, with purest pleasure—
    Star of morning, mystic rose.

Hymn: Her Name Is Grace

    Her name is Grace,
Her voice a silent song,
    A sheltering space
For those who suffer long.
    Her soothing hands
Can cool a fevered brow;
    She understands,
And who can tell us how?

    With touch so sweet,
She lifts a soul from gloom;
    Beneath her feet,
A wasteland starts to bloom.
    With veils of dew
She vests the clovered plain;
    And hope is new
Where darkness used to reign.

    Bright star of Love,
She shines with brilliance pure,
    Delightful dove
Whose blessing is secure:
    Pearl of great worth,
From age to endless age,
    Heaven and earth
Unite to sing her praise.

4

A Candle in the Gathering Gloom

A Look Askance at Spring

Softly, blossoms explode:
pink, white, lavender, sky-blue!
Delirious riot of floral superabundance!

But my inner canon lawyer has reservations.

Have they run all this exuberance
past Cardinal Stickler and Bishop Brusk?
Has all this bursting and blooming cleared the Curia?

Has the paperwork of the chestnut-tree,
liberal with impertinent burgeonings,
gone through the proper channels?

And what about the productions
of this fresh magnolia?
Are they reliable? Are they orthodox?

Has the sparrow, little pouch of mischief,
suspicious ounce of happiness,
obtained a *Nihil Obstat,*
an *Imprimatur?*

Where is the hyacinth's certificate,
the daffodil's documentation?

Nothing seems to be following
the carefully laid-out guidelines!
Isn't anyone else bothered by that?

Daughters

daughters who will never be unheavened
you have names that engender wonder

Hyacinth   Melpomene   October

in this world you establish charity
you wield sceptres of science

you enthrone yourselves in poetry

nations hang upon the promise of your praises
earth quakes at your tender condemnations

coffeehouses rejoice   cathedrals tremble
sidewalks ring and sing beneath your feet

blue comets blaze amid the hairs of your head

Amid Cold Churches

Amid cold churches and smashed beer-bottles,
teenage boy who hopes for something better,
you scrawl hot sonnets in the bothered room
of a triple-decker near an asphalt schoolyard.

Amid the strivings and the fled-from battles,
you sit on your bed and write a heart-hurt letter
to God, to a girl, to a boy, as darkness deepens
in a sky of balked desire and steel-bright stars.

Oh, dreamer of sixteen! Your ravenous mind
would learn all the languages. You would read
Death in Venice, Ginsberg, all the gay books
against which prim and preachy teachers cautioned.

East Boston streets: bare-knuckled, sticks and stones.
Jackets studded with heavy-metal badges,
streetwise icons at whom timid lads flinch,
the one kind girl who doesn't mock the brainiac.

Cigarettes secretly, shamelessly smoked, making
a crush's breath as sexy as rough foreplay,
as hasty humping on a mattress, in a phone-booth,
as four-letter words flung to make virgins blush.

Struck deep by Allison, struck deep by Johnny,
you saw *The Breakfast Club* twelve times, at least.
You told close friends how you were, who you were.
They guessed. They knew. And they had your back.

Confession with Jennifer

So, Tuesday morning, as if it were
the most natural thing in the world
for a cradle Catholic who until recently
had been a strident ecclesial partisan,
I asked Jennifer, an Episcopal priest,
if she'd consent to hear my confession.
She put her hand to her heart, so gently,
and smiled: "Yes, Thomas, it would be an honour."

Experts in Catholic canon law might object.
They can go sit on a cactus.
All my drive-through Saturday shrivings
in Roman precincts haven't helped one bit
to banish my self-focus, my despair.

I need to let my sister, my even-Christian,
into my guarded and unsolaced sorrows.
I will ask the Christ in Jennifer to bless me,
will tell her my tale of woe and of soul-blight,
surrender my mean doubts, my petty fears,
and trust in the embodiment of Grace.

Reconciliation

Confession with Jennifer
is all things lilac and lemon,
is feather-light, is Paul Verlaine,
is softness and the bobolink.
It lands as gentle as spirit-dust
on a sun-brightened lozenge
of an ancient parlour's carpet.
It refreshes. It fortifies.
It invigorates like January's
gape of a moon over snow-glaze.
It blazes like a hundred Julys.

Confession with Jennifer
is the fumbling grace
of a toddler, awake with life
and colour, loud with joy.
It is the gift of fences
toppled, of walls crumbling,
of a petrified heart being
coaxed back to tenderness.
Apogee and astonishment,
equinox and exultation.

God

a priest heard my confession yesterday
and told me that God isn't static
God is kinetic, God is Pentecost

she doesn't get moldy or mildewed
she will *flame out like shining from shook foil*
she will walk barefoot in damp June grass

God is the 11th Step and the Allston nooner
she is Dean Amy and the poets of Black Seed
she is every Jennifer whom I have ever known

she is the ladybug and Theodore Roethke
she is the hyacinth and Mary Oliver
she is the solacing 5 am barista
who calls me Jackie Onassis

she is acolyte and apostate, hierophant and heretic
she is humanity in all its glorious imperfection
she doesn't always know what will come next
she is wind and flame, love and rage
she is a candle in the gathering gloom

a black thorn stick in the hands of Seamus Heaney
a sparrow in the cell of St Kevin
a lake of beer in the precinct of St Brigid
a hazelnut in the hand of Blessed Julian

she is the cloister at Clonmacnoise
the rabbit bounding across the grass of Spencer

living water, spendthrift of mercy, healer of heartwounds
she gives life, she restores life, she is life in us

Portrait of the Oddest

I explain things
that really don't need explaining.
I remember the birthdays of college roommates,
not seen in 35 years.
Sometimes I'm Polonius. Sometimes I'm Cal Coolidge.

People scare me. As do many other things!
I prize autumn and praise Dylan Thomas.
I venerate Marianne Moore
for her Data-and-Spock-like essays.
I talk to myself in four different languages.

I gobble crackers, clutch my pillow,
and pray the word *belly* like a mantra.
I honour women, but am not Relationship Material.
I used to think I was an adult
because I drank like a pissed fish.

I like Matt, the rector of St James's Church.
I can make him laugh, the incorrigible rascal.
I often blurt out "My word!" and "Egad!"
I am easily astonished. I love the Virgin Mary.
I say my rosary and don't care who throws shade.

At gatherings in church basements,
I'm known as "the Peace & Light guy."
I always end my shares by saying
Peace and light, everyone—
thanks for listening!

Chestnut Street Episode

On my way to catch the 77
to church last Sunday, I saw Donna
standing in a soft drizzle and smoking.
She held a damp rectangle of cardboard
from a ripped-up box over her head.

Seeing me unshielded from the rain,
she waggled the cardboard and offered,
"Would you like to borrow my umbrella?"

"I'm good!" I answered back.
"I'm thin enough to walk between the raindrops!"

Blessed Space

A free society means being free of those who rule over you—to do the things you care about, your passions, your pastimes, your loves—to exult in that blessed space where politics doesn't intervene.
  —Andrew Sullivan, in "The Madness of King Donald,"
   nymag.com, February 10, 2017

In this blessed space,
narrow brick-paved lane
behind First Unitarian,
I walk with you.

In this blessed space,
table for two at the Kickstand,
I sit with you, and we laugh.

In this blessed space,
where squirrels scamper
toward leaves of preternatural green
underneath a blossom-birthing sun,
I sing to you in my old ham voice
that cracks on the high notes.

In this blessed space,
we repair the havoc of demagogues
by keeping silence.
As we sit together,
waters of gratitude
surge above the heart-brim.

In this blessed space,
room of light and art
and books and music,
you are the host,
I am the guest.

Nightpiece

I lulled my sore and antic heart to sleep
by whispering their name to the silence

What Is Love?

Refuge and adventure.
Hidden treasure, pearl of worth.
Full moon in winter,
plain and evident starlight.
Loosening a dear friend's sandals,
running fingers
through "sable tresses."
Solace and salvation
in the seethe and simmer
of a crush-prone summer.
Joy of helping, of being helped,
when life gets cumbrous and gnarly.
Music that leads you
through agonies of bliss,
a song that follows you
down the back alley,
into the basilica,
at barbershop and bakery,
follows you home
and asks to be adopted.
It is snow, first and final:
deep wide hush, so lavish,
so cold and pure and true,
luminous under the gaunt
and vigilant trees.
A poetfriend. A churchmate.
A sibling in your sober *sangha*.

What is love? Do you know?
It exists in the distracted,
in the distressed,
in the artist, in the activist,
yes, even in the grumble-puppy,
the incel, the rage-muffin.
Seeing traces of god-light
and grace, even there.
Love is being alert. Receptive.
It is Nazareth and Natalie Merchant,
a thirty-year-old nun,
an eighty-year-old bookseller.
It is William Blake and saxophone solos,
disco tunes, boogie on down.
It is the soup of the day
at your favourite diner,
warmth for belly and heart.
A YouTube memory
that makes you sob and rock
with irrepressible tears.
Blossom and burst of April,
blaze and cadence of fall.
It's the name you hold close,
that tender holy cherishable name
whispered to embracing darkness,
reverently, as one whispers
a secret, a prayer.
It is the journey, always the journey.
It is this place. It is this moment.
Destination and desire,
hope and harbour and home.

Notes

"This Unbidden Love": The first draft of this poem dates from December 1985, when the author was sixteen.

"Contributor's Note": Guerric of Igny (+1157) was a Cistercian abbot, the Cistercians being monks in the Benedictine tradition.

"Speak Again, Bright Angel": *Verkakte,* Yiddish for "crappy." *Oysgeshpilt*: "exhausted, spent." *Geh schlafen:* "go to sleep."

"New Directions Paperbook 316": *Collected Poems* by Dylan Thomas. Laugharne (pronounced "larn") was the town in Wales where Thomas lived in the 1940s and early '50s. This poem contains many allusions and references to the work of Dylan Thomas.

"Eighties Soundtrack": *Sparkle in the Rain,* album by Simple Minds; *Low-life,* by New Order; *Hatful of Hollow,* by The Smiths

"Your Milwaukee": Rochambo and Stone Creek are the names of coffee-shops in East Milwaukee.

"After My First Visit": Rocket Baby is a bakery in Wauwatosa, Wisconsin. Atwater Beach is along Lake Michigan, in Shorewood, Wisconsin. Ted's Ice Cream is an establishment in Wauwatosa; Trinity Church is an Episcopal parish in the same town. Matt Talbot (1856–1925) was an Irish Catholic currently venerated by the Church as a patron of alcoholics; a recovery center in Milwaukee is named for him. "The 414" is a reference to Milwaukee's telephone area-code. Boswell Book Company is a bookstore on North Downer Avenue in Milwaukee. Freya: Elena's dog.

"At Half Past Five": "Honey-dipped," an old Boston regionalism for a glazed donut.

"Paulist Center": In the language of English mystic Julian of Norwich (c. 1342–1416), an "even-Christian" is a fellow-Christian. See also "Confession with Jennifer."

"Vespers": Cooke's Hollow is a small public park in Arlington, MA.

"Wisdom": Written in the metre of "Praise my soul, the King of heaven" by Scottish hymnographer Henry Francis Lyte (1793–1847). In this hymn, as in "Her Name Is Grace," I am trying to find female, non-patriarchal, images of divinity.

"A Look Askance at Spring": In the Roman Catholic Church, the Curia is a board of appointed cardinals who advise the Pope, much like a presidential cabinet. Catholic publishers will sometimes use the Latin phrases *nihil obstat* ("nothing stands against") and *imprimatur* ("it may be printed") to indicate that a book accords with magisterial doctrine.

"Daughters": In Greek mythology, Melpomene is the muse of tragedy.

"God": *flame out like shining from shook foil,* see "God's Grandeur" by Gerard Manley Hopkins (1844–89).

"Blessed Space": The Kickstand is an Arlington, Massachusetts coffeehouse.

"What Is Love?": *Sangha:* assembly, community (Sanskrit).

About the Author

Thomas DeFreitas was educated at the Boston Latin School. His poems have appeared in *Dappled Things, The Orchards Poetry Journal, Ovunque Siamo, Pensive,* and elsewhere.

In 2018, Thomas's poem "Chasing the Waves" was chosen by Arlington (MA) Poet Laureate Cathie Desjardins to be part of the Talking Chair Project, a poetry exhibit at the Robbins Library in Arlington. In the summer of 2019, "Detox" was chosen as an Award Poem by the editors of *Plainsongs*. In November 2024, Thomas's poem "Grief," found in this volume, was nominated for a Pushcart Prize by the editor of *Autumn Sky Poetry Daily*.

Thomas's three previous collections have all been published by Kelsay Books: *Swift River Ballad* (2023), *Longfellow, Tell Me* (2022), and *Winter in Halifax* (2021). Thomas's work has also been included in *On and Off the Road: Poems of New Hampshire* (Peterborough Poetry Project, 2020) and *The 2017 Poetry Marathon Anthology,* edited by Caitlin and Jacob Jans.

Thomas is a member of St. James's Episcopal Church, Cambridge, MA, where on All Saints Sunday 2023 he preached a sermon at the invitation of the rector, Rev. Matthew W. Stewart, and where he has collaborated with music minister Patrick G. Michaels on several hymns that have been sung at Sunday liturgies.

Resident of Arlington, MA since 2010, Thomas is a contributing member of the Academy of American Poets. He is also active in the New England Poetry Club, Boston's Black Seed Writers, and Arlington's Beehive Poetry Group.

His website is:
thomasdefreitas.me